Joseph Thomas Robert

A parliamentary syllabus

Twenty-four progressive lessons in parliamentary practice for high

schools, colleges, literary clubs, etc

Joseph Thomas Robert

A parliamentary syllabus
*Twenty-four progressive lessons in parliamentary practice for high schools,
colleges, literary clubs, etc*

ISBN/EAN: 9783337150952

Printed in Europe, USA, Canada, Australia, Japan

Cover: Foto ©Paul-Georg Meister /pixelio.de

More available books at **www.hansebooks.com**

A

·PARLIAMENTARY SYLLABUS·

TWENTY-FOUR PROGRESSIVE LESSONS IN PARLIA-
MENTARY PRACTICE FOR HIGH SCHOOLS,
COLLEGES, LITERARY CLUBS, ETC.

BY JOSEPH T. ROBERT,

PRINCIPAL, THE ROBERT SCHOOL OF PARLIAMENTARY LAW,
CHICAGO, ILL.

CHICAGO
SCOTT, FORESMAN & CO.
1897

PRESS OF ROGERS & SMITH CO., CHICAGO.

PREFACE.

THIS little book is not designed to take the place of, but rather to introduce the student to, larger works. Many rules given may seem so simple as not to need stating. The author's experience in conducting classes of College and Law Students, Chautauquas, Men's and Women's Clubs, etc., has taught him that nothing hinders progress more than misunderstanding the simple things at the beginning, and that nothing is more common.

The Syllabus is written especially for that large and growing class of Clubs, Literary Societies, etc., which so deeply feel the need of a better acquaintance with Parliamentary forms and usages, as well as the difficulties in the way of gaining such practical knowledge through mere individual study, that they are turning resolutely to Club Practice as the true and only solution of this problem. It is hoped that in such Club Practice—*practice with study*—these lessons will be found helpful and not too difficult.

Lesson XXIV, on Reversal of Action on Amendments, contains, the author believes, the only complete statement given to the public of this most perplexing of all Parliamentary Laws, and is given in answer to many requests.

References to other works are made where the rule given might be thought an innovation. On a few points, without authoritative rule or precedent, the endorsement of the rule here given by the author of " Robert's Rules " is indicated by "H. M. R."

These Lessons will be doubly helpful if each Syllabus is used for Club-Drill at two separate sessions of one to two hours each.

The writer takes pleasure in acknowledging the invaluable aid derived from years of interchange of opinions and rulings in submitted cases, as well as frequent discussions of obscure and controverted points, with his brother, Col. H. M. Robert, the author of "Robert's Rules of Order."

JOSEPH T. ROBERT.

CHICAGO, ILL., October, 1897.

TABLE OF CONTENTS.

LESSON

I. TEMPORARY ORGANIZATION.—How to call a Meeting to Order. Who is in control. What Title and Power. ELECTIONS. How offer Resolutions. A Question Stated. OBTAINING THE FLOOR. MOTIONS—making and seconding. Things to Avoid. Things to Do. POINT OF ORDER.

II. AMEND.—Five Forms. How Move. Six Laws. "Not." "Germane." "Hostile." "Trivial."
PREVIOUS QUESTION. Means Three Things—*a child can understand and apply*. Previous Question, *Limited*.

III. AMEND (*continued*).—Five Laws. Can an Amendment always be amended? Can a Motion? Amendment to Amendment? "*Separate.*" Debatable? Order of voting on Resolution and Amendments. Unamendable Motions. PARLIAMENTARY INQUIRY. DOUBTING THE VOTE. *Call for Division*.

IV. QUESTION OF CONSIDERATION.—"I object." Applies? When made? Ten simple Laws. Obnoxious Questions. Second? *Question reversed in stating*. A Back-handed Two-thirds Vote.
PRINCIPAL MOTIONS—briefly defined. CLOSE DEBATE (*part 1*).

V. LAY ON THE TABLE.—Use and Abuse. Laws. Tabling Amendments. Effect on Main Question. Limits. "Vitally connected." Reconsider. TAKE FROM THE TABLE.—Laws and Forms. RECESS. Order of Precedence.

VI. INDEFINITELY POSTPONE.—Yields to? Precedes? Object. Forms. POSTPONE DEFINITELY.
RECONSIDER (*part 1*).—Who can move? "*Prevailing side.*"

VII. APPEALS.—What Decisions can be appealed from? "Personally affected." Effect of Tabling. Tie Vote. Can Chairman vote? Debatable or Undebatable? *Question reversed*. Twelve Laws.

VIII. WITHDRAWAL OF A MOTION.—What may be Withdrawn? When? Why? Consent of Second. General Consent. Motion to Allow. Forms and Rules.

IX. AMEND BY DIVISION.—Twelve Plain Rules. Who decides how? Mover *vs.* Chairman. "Independent." Stand Alone. Mode of Action. Order of , Voting. What can't be Divided? A Better Way. Forms.

X. SUBSTITUTE.—Is an Amendment. Strike out and Insert on a Larger Scale. When in Order. Difficult Problems. Common Mistakes.

XI. PERMANENT ORGANIZATION.—Add *pro tem*. State Object. Formal Resolution. Committee on Constitution. True Way to Amend and Adopt. "Adopt Article" ruled out. Suspend Rules.

5

LESSON

XII. ELECTION OF OFFICERS.—Tellers' Work and Reports of Ballots. Voting for One not Nominated. Blanks Counted? Imperfect Ballots—how treated. WHO IS ELECTED? Chairman's Action. INFORMAL BALLOT.

XIII. ORDER OF BUSINESS.—Adjourn in Order? Special Order. Taking up Business out of Proper Order. SUSPENSION OF RULES. QUORUM.

XIV. MINUTES.—Effect of Subsidary Motions on "Amend Minutes." *Rank* of Minutes. "Approve" by General Consent, or Motion. How late can Minutes be Corrected? Should contain what?

XV. QUESTIONS OF PRIVILEGE.—What are? Rank. If requiring Immediate Action. Chair. Forms for Members and Chairman. Rules. Janitor. Tellers. Rights of New Members. CHANGING A VOTE.

XVI. COMMIT AND COMMITTEES.—Work of. How Appointed? Nominated? Elected? Rules and Forms. Committee of the Whole. Standing and Select Committees. Sub-committees. Instructing. Amending.

XVII. ADJOURN.—Qualified. Unqualified. What is in Order while Adjourn is pending? Six Forms of Adjourn. Adjourn *sine die* debatable. Adjourn *at* and *to* a Time and *to* a Place.

XVIII. RECONSIDER—*(more fully treated)*. Who can Move? "Prevailing side" may be Minority. Second? Who? When? Effect. In what order Reconsider Motion, Amendment, and Amendment to Amendment?

XIX. FIX TIME (AND PLACE) TO WHICH TO ADJOURN.—When Another Question is pending. When not. Two Questions of very different Rank. Don't combine Fix Time and Adjourn. Forms and Rules.

XX. EXTEND, LIMIT AND CLOSE DEBATE.—Apply to? Rank. Two-thirds Vote. Amend and Debate? Exact Scope of Each. Length and Number of Speeches. Length of Debate. Time Limit reached.

XXI. PREVIOUS QUESTION—*(more fully stated)*. Previous Question Limited and without Limit. PREVIOUS QUESTION AND RECONSIDER. Previous Question in Force. Previous Question Exhausted. Votes under Previous Question Reconsidered in both cases.

XXII. SUSPEND RULES, BY-LAWS, CONSTITUTION.—Two-thirds Vote. Can Suspend what By-Laws and Rules? Principles, Laws, Precedence, can not be Suspended. Rules of Superior Bodies.

XXIII. AMEND RULES, BY-LAWS, ETC.—When? After what Notice? Two-thirds Vote? "Germane" enforced. Amend Amendment by Majority? U. S., State, Ecclesiastical and Fraternity Laws. INCORPORATION.

XXIV. TO REVERSE ACTION ON AMENDMENTS.—To Insert, *lost*. To Insert, *carried*. Strike out, *lost*. Strike out, *carried*. Strike out and Insert, *lost or carried*. *In all*, TWENTY-FOUR RULES. Examples.

TABLES OF MOTIONS.

I. MOTIONS WHICH CAN NOT BE RECONSIDERED.

1 Adjourn.
2 Election to office of a person present and not declining.
3 Lay on the Table; *affirmative vote.*
4 Previous Question (affirmative vote), *if partly or wholly executed.*
5 A Question already Reconsidered, *unless amended during first Reconsideration.*

6 A Question, to Reconsider which has already been moved and lost.
7 Reconsider.
8 Recess.
9 Suspend Rules.
10 Take from the Table; *affirmative vote.*
11 A Vote, as a result of which something has been done which the Assembly can not reverse.

II. QUESTIONS WHICH CAN NOT BE AMENDED. See LESSON III.

III. UNDEBATABLE QUESTIONS.

1 Amendments to Undebatable Questions.
2 Adjourn (unqualified).
3 Adjourn, Fix Time to which to, (Priv'd).*
4 Appeals, relating to Indecorum, Transgression of Rules of Debate, Priority of Business; or made during pendency of any undebatable question.
5 Call to Order.
6 Close Debate.
7 Doubting the Vote.
8 Extend Limits of Debate.
9 Fix Time to which to Adjourn, (Priv'd).*
10 General Consent, asking for.
11 Lay on the Table.
12 Leave to Continue after Indecorum.
13 Limit Debate.
14 Motions made while Previous Question or any Undebatable Question is pending.†
15 Object to Consideration.

16 Object, where General Consent is required.
17 Orders of the Day, call for.
18 Postpone to a Definite Time.‡
19 Point of Order.
20 Precedence of Motions, Questions as to.
21 Previous Question.
22 Priority of Business, Questions relating to.
23 Reading Papers.
24 Recess.
25 Reconsider an Undebatable Q'n.
26 Enter "Reconsider" on Minutes.
27 Rise (in Committee—Adjourn).
28 Substitute for Undebatable Q'n.
29 Suspend Rules.
30 Take from the Table.
31 Take up Question out of its Proper Order.
32 Vote, Changing a.
33 Voting, Questions as to Mode of.
34 " Call for Division in.
35 Withdrawal of a Motion.
36 " " Second.

* "Fix Time to which to Adjourn" is Unprivileged and Debatable, *if moved when no other question is pending.*
† II. M. R.
‡ Allows only limited debate on Postpone.

9

LISTS OF MOTIONS.

I.	PRIVILEGED QUESTIONS.	III.	SUBSIDIARY QUESTIONS.
1	Fix the Time to which to Adjourn.	1	Lay on the Table.
2	Adjourn (unqualified).	2	Previous Question.
3	Take a Recess.	3	Close and Limit Debate.
4	Questions of Privilege.	4	Extend Limits of Debate.
5	Call for Orders of the Day.	5	Postpone Definitely.
		6	Commit or Refer.
II.	**INCIDENTAL QUESTIONS.**	7	Amend.
1	Questions of Order.	8	Postpone Indefinitely.
2	Appeal.		
3	Objection to Consideration.		
4	Questions as to Mode of Voting.		
5	Enter Reconsider on Minutes.		
6	Reading Papers.		
7	Withdraw a Motion.		
8	Suspend Rules.		

ABBREVIATIONS.

Fix Time—Fix the Time to which to Adjourn.
H. M. R.—H. M. Robert, author of Robert's Rules.
P. Q.   —Previous Question.
R. R.   —Robert's Rules of Order.

11

A PARLIAMENTARY SYLLABUS.

TWENTY-FOUR PROGRESSIVE LESSONS.

SYLLABUS — LESSON I.

TEMPORARY ORGANIZATION — MOTIONS — POINT OF ORDER.

I. ORGANIZATION OF AN OCCASIONAL MEETING.
1. At the appointed time some one should come forward and say: The meeting will please come to order. I move that Mr. A. act as Chairman. (If not promptly seconded, say: Is the motion seconded?)
2. It is moved and seconded that Mr. A. act as Chairman. Are you ready for the question? (Waiting an instant)—All in favor of the motion will say *aye* ; (after ayes respond) those opposed, *no.*
3. The *ayes* have it, Mr. A. is elected and will please take the Chair (or, the *noes* have it, the motion is lost and nominations for Chairman are in order).
4. "Nominations for Chairman are in order" may be used as soon as the meeting is called to order (1).

II. OBTAINING THE FLOOR.
1. Before making a motion or speech a member must Obtain the Floor; *i. e.* rise, address the Chair, and wait till recognized.
2. The Chair recognizes by naming the member: *e. g.* "Mr. Jones."
3. "Mr. Chairman," "Mrs. or Miss (or Madam) Chairman" are the usual forms. If a special title belongs to the office, that should be used, as "Mr. Speaker," "Mrs. President."

III. MAKING AND SECONDING MOTIONS.
1. Don't say "I motion," "I move you," "I move the Chair."
2. Obtain the floor and say "I move," stating the motion briefly.
3. In Seconding a motion don't say "I sustain" or "I support the motion."
4. Remain seated, without addressing the Chair, and say: "I second the motion" (or Appeal, etc.).—R. R.

IV. RESOLUTIONS.
1. Should be read and handed to the Chair or Secretary.
   Forms: I move the adoption of the following resolution: Resolved, That etc.

V. POINT OF ORDER.
1. If a member sees any violation of the rules he may (even while another has the floor) rise and say: "Mr. Chairman, I rise to a Point of Order."
2. Chairman: "Please state the point of order."
3. Chairman: "The Chair decides the point (not) well taken, and the member must speak to the pending amendment."
4. The Chairman can himself call a member to order.

SYLLABUS—LESSON II.

AMEND—FIVE FORMS—HOSTILE AND GERMANE—PREVIOUS QUESTION.

I. FIVE FORMS OF AMENDMENT.
  1. To insert or add.
  2. To strike out.   } See also Lesson III.
  3. To strike out and insert.
  4. To substitute. (Lesson X.)
  5. To divide. (Lesson IX.)

II. LAWS — GERMANE, HOSTILE, TRIVIAL.
  1. An Amendment may be Hostile (*i. e.* directly opposed to the original motion); but must be Germane (*i. e.* have a direct bearing on the subject of the original motion).
  2. An Amendment *obviously Trivial* should be ruled out by the Chair: *e. g.* " I move to amend by adding ' Queen Victoria ' to the committee."
  3. An Amendment is debatable only when the main question is debatable.
  4. The words Inserted or Struck Out must be connected words.
  5. In " Strike out and Insert," the words must be inserted *in the place from which the others were struck out.—R. R.*
  6. To " Strike out and Insert " is one motion, and can not be divided.

III. FORMS.
  1. I move to amend the amendment by inserting the words "by law" after the word "prohibited."
  2. I move to amend the second resolution by striking out the word "taxpayers," and inserting the words "able to read."
  3. The ayes (noes) have it, and the amendment is adopted (or lost).
  4. The question now recurs on the resolution as amended (*or, if the amendment fails,* on the original resolution). Are you ready for the question?

IV. PREVIOUS QUESTION. (*For fuller treatment, see Lesson XXI.*)
  1. The Previous Question means: *Stop debating, stop amending, and vote.*
  2. It brings the pending question or questions to an immediate vote.
  3. The Previous Question may be limited by its mover to one or more questions.
  4. Requires a two-thirds vote.

V. FORMS.
  1. I move the Previous Question (on the amendment).
  2. Shall the main question be now put?
  3. Shall the question be now put on the amendment?
  4. Two-thirds voting in the affirmative, the *ayes* have it, and the. Previous Question is ordered (on the amendments).

  NOTE.—Unless all members of the Assembly are familiar with Parliamentary Law, *it is best,* if a motion requires a two-thirds vote, *to announce that fact:* (*a*) In stating the question, and (*b*) In announcing the result.

SYLLABUS — LESSON III.

AMEND (Part 2) — PARLIAMENTARY INQUIRY — DOUBTING THE VOTE.

I. LAWS OF AMENDMENTS.
   1. Every amendment can be amended.
   2. An amendment to an amendment can not be amended.
   3. Two separate amendments can not be before an Assembly at the same time.
   4. When a motion, an amendment and an amendment to the amendment are pending, the vote is taken—
      (a) On the amendment to the amendment.
      (b) On the amendment (or, if amended, on *the amendment as amended*).
      (c) On the original motion (or, if amended, on *the motion as amended*).

II. The following are the principal questions which can not be amended:
   1. Adjourn.*
   2. Appeal.
   3. Lay on (and Take from) the Table.
   4. Leave to continue speaking, etc.
   5. Object to Consideration.
   6. Orders of the Day, call for.
   7. Postpone Indefinitely.
   8. Previous Question.
   9. Reconsider.
   10. Suspend Rules.
   11. Take up business out of order.
   12. Withdrawal of a motion.

III. PARLIAMENTARY INQUIRY.
   1. If a member is in doubt as to any rule, method or form, relating to *business already before the Assembly*, or *which he wishes to bring up* for consideration:
   2. He should rise and say: " Mr. Chairman, I rise to a Parliamentary Inquiry."
   3. Chairman: " Please state the Inquiry."
   4. Needs neither recognition by the Chair, nor a second.

IV. DOUBTING THE VOTE AND DIVISION.
   1. If any member is not satisfied with the result (as stated by the Chair) of any vote by ayes and noes, he may rise and say: "Mr. Chairman, I doubt the vote (or, Mr. Chairman, I call for a Division)."
   2. Chairman: "A division is called for. All in favor will rise and stand until counted ; (after counting) those opposed will rise."
   3. The Chair may count, or ask the Secretary, or appoint Tellers from both sides.
   4. The number may be announced by the Chair as each side is counted, or after both sides have voted, e. g. 25 in the affirmative, 40 in the negative, and the motion is lost.

* " Adjourn " always means " ADJOURN, *Unqualified*," unless otherwise stated.

SYLLABUS — LESSON IV.

OBJECT TO CONSIDERATION — CLOSE DEBATE. (*See* LESSON XX.)

I. OBJECT TO CONSIDERATION:
   1. Applies only to Principal Motions (*i. e.* motions introducing a subject).
   2. Must be made before debate, amendment or other motion, but after the question has been stated by the Chair.
   3. The Chair can put the question without a motion, if he thinks best.
   4. Is in order when another has the floor.
   5. Needs no recognition or second.
   6. Can not be debated, amended, or have any other subsidiary motion applied to it, except:
   7. Can be laid on the table, *carrying the main question with it.*
   8. A *two-thirds vote in the negative* defeats Consideration for the entire session, unless reconsidered.
   9. An affirmative vote of more than one-third leaves the question before the Assembly for action.

II. FORMS.
   1. Mr. Chairman, I object to the consideration of the question (petition, **etc.**).
   2. Objection to consideration being made, the question before the Assembly is, "Shall the question be considered? A two-thirds negative vote is required to prevent consideration. Are you ready for the question?"
   3. All in favor of consideration will say *aye;* those opposed, *no.*
   4. More than one-third voting in the affirmative, the ayes have it and the question (report, etc.) is before the Assembly for consideration.
   5. Two-thirds voting in the negative, the noes have it and the Assembly refuses to consider.

III. CLOSE DEBATE. (*See Lesson XX.*)
   1. Applies to all debatable questions.
   2. Can not be debated.
   3. Can be amended and reconsidered.
   4. At the time fixed, cuts off debate and amendments and brings the question or questions to which it is applied, to a vote.
   5. Applies to a motion and its amendments, unless limited by the mover.
   6. Requires a two-thirds vote.

IV. FORMS.
   1. I move that the debate be *now* closed (or, closed at 10:30).
   2. I move to amend by striking out "thirty."
   3. Two-thirds voting in the affirmative, the ayes have it, and debate will close at 10:30.

SYLLABUS — LESSON V.

LAY ON THE TABLE—TAKE FROM THE TABLE—RECESS.

I. LAY ON THE TABLE:
1. Tabling any question tables every other vitally connected question ; *e. g.* Amendment tabled, carries the main question to the table.   ·
2. Can not be debated or amended.
3. Yields to all Privileged and Incidental Questions, except Object.
4. *Carried,* can not be Reconsidered, but question must be Taken from the Table.
5. *Lost,* can be Reconsidered, before the question is changed (by amendment, etc.) ; after such change it must be Renewed.

II. APPARENT EXCEPTIONS TO ABOVE RULES.
Tabling the following questions Tables nothing else :
1. Amendment to Minutes.
2. Amendment to Rules (etc.) already adopted. .
3. Appeal (sustains the Chair).
4. Reconsider..
5. Question of Privilege.
6. Repeal, Rescind, Expunge.

III. THE FOLLOWING QUESTIONS CAN NOT BE LAID ON THE TABLE:
1. Adjourn.
2. Fix Time (Privileged).
3. Lay on the Table.
4. Orders of the Day (as a class).
5. Priority of Business (questions as to).
6. Take from the Table.

IV. TAKE FROM THE TABLE.
1. Rules I, 1–3 apply also to Take from the Table
2. Questions Laid on the Table can be Taken from the Table during the same session, when no other question is pending.
3. In organizations with sessions not longer than a day, and as often as monthly, *the best practice is* to allow any question to be taken from the Table which was Laid on the Table at the previous session.—R. R.
4. Take from the Table: (*a*) *Lost,* can be Reconsidered ; (*b*) *Carried,* can not be Reconsidered ; but the question can be again Laid on the Table.

V. FORMS.
1. I move the question be Laid on the Table.
2. I move the report of the Social Committee be Taken from the Table.

VI. RECESS.
1. Precedes all questions except Fix Time (Privileged) and Adjourn.
2. Can not be debated. Can be amended.
3. The "meeting" after a Recess *is not another but the same* "meeting."

VII. FORMS.
1. I move we now take a Recess of one hour (or, till 7 P. M.).

SYLLABUS — LESSON VI.

POSTPONE INDEFINITELY — POSTPONE DEFINITELY — PART I OF RECONSIDER.

I. POSTPONE INDEFINITELY:
  1. Applies only to—
     (a) Principal Motions, *i. e.* Motions introducing a subject.
     (b) Questions of Privilege.
  2. Yields to all Privileged, Incidental and Subsidiary Questions, except:
     (a) Objection to Consideration.
     (b) Amend.
  3. Can be debated, and opens the main question to debate.
  4. Can not be amended.
  5. Can be reconsidered.

II. EFFECT OF POSTPONE INDEFINITELY AND RELATED MOTIONS.
  1. The Previous Question and Close Debate, if ordered, apply only to Postpone.
  2. Lay on the Table, Commit and Postpone Definitely, applied to Postpone Indefinitely, carry the main question also.
  3. Postpone Indefinitely *carried*, puts aside the question for the entire session, unless reconsidered.
  4. Postpone Indefinitely *lost,* leaves the main question before the Assembly just as it was.

III. FORMS.
  1. I move the question (of Privilege) be Indefinitely Postponed.

IV. POSTPONE DEFINITELY (*i. e.* TO A CERTAIN TIME).
  1. Can be Amended, Tabled, Reconsidered.
  2. Precedes Commit, Amend, Indefinitely Postpone.
  3. Allows limited debate, including the main question only so far as it relates to the propriety of postponement.
  4. A question can be postponed to any time during the session, or to the next session, and then it is included in Unfinished Business.
  5. Previous Question (unless limited to Postpone) applies to the main question also.

V. FORMS.
  1. I move the question be postponed to the next meeting.

VI. PART I OF RECONSIDER. (*More fully treated in Lesson XVIII.*)
  1. Reconsider must be moved (except when the vote was by ballot) by one who voted on the prevailing (*winning*) side. Any one can second it.
  2. Reconsider must be moved on the same day, or the next.
  3. Is debatable, when the main question is.
  4. When debatable opens the main question to debate.

VII. FORMS.
  1. I move to Reconsider (the vote on) the amendment.
     NOTE.—For questions which can not be Reconsidered, see page 7.

SYLLABUS — LESSON VII.

APPEAL.

I. APPEAL.

1. Every decision of the Chair can be appealed from, except decisions made while another appeal is pending.
2. Any member, even if personally affected by the decision, can appeal.
3. Must be seconded ("I second the appeal").
4. An Appeal can not be amended.
5. Tabling an Appeal does not table the main question, but sustains the Chair till the Appeal is taken from the table and acted on.
6. Previous Question and Close Debate, applied to Appeal, do not affect the main question.
7. Reconsidering an Appeal does not Reconsider the main question.
8. A Tie-vote sustains the Chair, *even if caused by the vote of the Chairman.*— R. R. (See Note.)
9. The Chair is not obliged to decide a Point of Order, or Question of Privilege. May avoid friction and Appeal by at once putting such questions to vote without a motion. (FORMS 6, 7.)
10. *Appeals are Undebatable*, if relating to:
    (*a*) Indecorum.
    (*b*) Rules of Debate.
    (*c*) Priority of Business; or:
    (*d*) If made while any undebatable question is pending.—H. M. R.
11. If debatable, no member shall speak more than once.
12. Whether debatable or not, the Chairman has the right to state the reasons for his decision (without leaving the chair), before putting the question on the appeal.

II. FORMS.

1. I appeal from the decision of the Chair. (I second the appeal.)
2. Chairman: The decision of the Chair is appealed from. The question is, Shall the decision of the Chair stand as the judgment of the Assembly? Are you ready for the question?
3. Chairman: All in favor of sustaining the decision of the Chair, say *aye*, etc.
4. Chairman: The *ayes* have it, and the decision of the Chair is sustained.
5. Chairman: The *noes* have it, and the decision of the Chair is overruled.
6. The Chair is in doubt. All who believe the amendment to be in order, say *aye*, etc. (See 9, above.)
7. The ayes have it, and the Assembly has decided the amendment to be in order. The question now recurs on the adoption of the amendment, striking out the word "Railways" and inserting "Corporations." Are you ready, etc.?

NOTE.—The rule is: The Chair can vote *whenever his vote would change the result*—also in balloting, and voting by *yeas* and *nays*. In the latter case, the Chairman's name should be called last.

SYLLABUS — LESSON VIII.

WITHDRAWAL OF A MOTION.

I. BEFORE A MOTION IS STATED, the maker can, *with consent of the second :*
  1. Withdraw, amend or completely change, *any question.*
  2. If the second objects, withdrawal fails, and the Chair states the question.

II. AFTER A QUESTION IS STATED, and before it is affected by amendment or other motion:
  1. The maker can Withdraw, Amend or Substitute—by *general consent.*
  2. If any one objects, Leave to Withdraw, etc., may be granted:
    (a) By formal motion and vote.
    (b) Informally, by vote without motion.
  3. Withdrawal may be made at (or without) the suggestion of the Chair, or other member, who *may give very briefly reasons for such request.*
  4. All motions and requests relating to Withdrawal, etc., are undebatable.

III. OBJECTS AND EFFECTS OF WITHDRAWAL.
  1. If withdrawal fails, the question to which it applied, remains before the Assembly.
  2. A motion withdrawn, is as if it had never been made.
  3. Objects: To cut off burning topics; give way to urgent business; relieve the mover of responsibility; amend most easily and quickly; change unamendable motions ; *e. g.* withdraw *Adjourn* and move *Recess.*

IV. FORMS.
  1. (Obtaining the floor). I wish to withdraw the motion.
  2. I wish the member would withdraw the motion so as to allow the Report, etc.
  3. I wish the member would amend the instructions so that the Committee, etc.
  4. (Before the motion is stated by the Chair). Chairman: Does the second consent?
  5. (After the question is stated by the Chair). Chairman: Is there any objection?
  6. Chairman: There being no objection, the motion is withdrawn (amended).
  7. I move the gentleman be allowed to withdraw the motion.
  8. (When a member wishes to withdraw a motion, and there is objection.) *Chairman, without waiting for a motion to allow, etc., may say:* Shall the member be granted leave, etc.? All in favor, etc. The ayes have it, and the motion is withdrawn.

SYLLABUS — LESSON IX.

AMEND BY DIVISION.

I. AMEND BY DIVISION.

1. The Division of a question is a form of amendment used to secure separate votes on different parts of a motion or resolution.
2. All laws which apply to other amendments, apply also to Division.
3. No member can insist upon the division of any question.
4. The Chairman has no more right to decide *how* a motion or resolution shall be divided, than to decide the form of any other amendment.
5. A Division must be made on a *motion specifying how the question is to be divided.*
6. A motion to Divide can be amended, as to—
   (a) The number of parts into which the question is to be divided.
   (b) The place where each part ends.
7. The parts into which a question is divided must be so independent that an Assembly can act upon either, if all the other parts fail.
8. Instead of dividing a question the same result can usually be better reached by some other form of amendment.
9. If the motion to divide is carried each part is treated as an independent motion or resolution, *i. e.* the first part is debated, amended and *fully disposed of,* before the second part can be considered.
10. The following can not be divided:
    (a) A motion and its amendments.
    (b) To Commit and Instruct.
    (c) To Strike out and Insert.
    (d) A Preamble can not be divided from the Resolutions it introduces.

II. FORMS.

1. I move to divide the resolution into three parts, the first ending with the word "franchise," and the second with the word "audited."
   NOTE.—Since the last part *must end* with the last word of the resolution, that ending should not be included in the motion to divide.
2. The ayes have it and the resolution is divided into three parts. The question now recurs on the first part, " Resolved, That mugwumps are the hope of the nation." Are you ready for the question?

SYLLABUS — LESSON X.

SUBSTITUTE.

I. A SUBSTITUTE:

   1. Is an amendment, and subject to all laws of amendments.

   2. Is *Strike out and Insert* on a larger scale.

   3. Substitutes another paragraph, resolution, article, report, etc., *on the same subject*, for the one pending.

   4. Where only a few words are changed it is best to use the form *Strike out and Insert*. (Lesson II.)

   5. A Substitute may be amended, but an amendment to a Substitute can not be amended.

   6. A Substitute for an amendment may be offered, and is treated as any other amendment to an amendment.

   7. While an amendment is pending, a Substitute *can not be offered* for the resolution (or part of it), or for the resolution and amendment (R. R.); but the amendment must first be voted on, and then (whether the amendment be carried or lost) a Substitute for the resolution will be in order.

   8. A Substitute is debatable if the main question is.

   9. The following questions applied to a Substitute cover the main question also:

      (*a*) Lay on the Table.

      (*b*) Postpone to a Certain Time.

      (*c*) Commit.

      (*d*) Previous Question (unless limited).

      (*e*) Close Debate (unless limited).

  10. Postpone Indefinitely is not in order while a Substitute is pending.

II. FORMS.

   1. I move to substitute for the amendment the following words: "Whenever a majority of the tax-payers shall make such a request, etc."

   2. I move the adoption of the following (as a) substitute for the fourth resolution: "Resolved, That we repudiate, etc.".

   NOTE.—The most important and most difficult rules to apply to Substitutes are adapted from Lesson II:

     1. A Substitute may be Hostile (*i. e.* directly opposed) to the original motion;

     2. But *must be* GERMANE, *i. e.* have a *direct bearing on the subject* of the original motion.

SYLLABUS — LESSON XI.

PERMANENT ORGANIZATION — CONSTITUTION.

I. TEMPORARY ORGANIZATION, ETC.
1. Organize as in Lesson I, adding "pro tem" to "Chairman" and "Sec."
2. The Chairman may (call on some one to) state the object of the meeting.
3. Some one may move the adoption of a resolution of this kind: "Resolved, That it is the sense of this meeting that a Current Events Club should be formed, etc."; which can be debated, amended and put to vote.
4. (After this vote, or omitting 2 or 3, or both.) A member should say: I move a Committee of (3) on Constitution (and By-Laws) be appointed by the Chair, to report as soon as possible.
5. The Committee may report at once a Constitution already prepared, or the Assembly may now adjourn, and hear the report at the next meeting.
6. The Chair, when notified that the Committee is ready, announces that the Assembly will now hear the report.

II. ADOPTION OF CONSTITUTION.
1. The Report should be read by the Chairman of the Committee (or Chairman or Secretary of the Assembly).
2. Member: "I move the adoption of the Constitution as reported." (Second.)
3. "It is moved and seconded that the Constitution as read be adopted. Are you ready for the question?"
4. The Chairman should then read Article I, and ask: "Are there any Amendments to Article I." (If Article is divided, read one Section at a time.)
5. After amendments and debate on this Article, the Chair should ask: "Are there any other amendments to Article I?" If not, read the other Articles in their order, *voting on the Amendments to each Article* (or Section) before reading the next.
6. No amendment is in order (during this reading) except to the Article (or Section) last read.
7. *A motion to adopt a reported Article* (or Section) is not in order.
8. *A motion to adopt an additional Article* (or Section) is not in order. In this case the proper form is: "I move to amend the Constitution by adding (inserting) the following: 'ARTICLE VII, *Quorum*, etc.'"
9. After separately reading and amending all the Articles in their order, the *Constitution as amended* should be read, when all parts are open to amendments and debate.
10. The Chair then puts the question on the adoption of the Constitution as amended.
11. After adopting a Constitution no business is in order except Adjourn and Recess; to enable intending members to comply with the conditions of membership; *e. g.* sign the Constitution—pay initiation fee.
12. By a two-thirds vote this order may be suspended, and the whole Constitution be read, debated and open to amendment.—R. R.
13. Members joining a Society before the first roll-call or business meeting are *exempt from conditions of membership at that time impossible; e. g.* rules requiring names to be recommended by two members, endorsed by Committee on Membership, etc., do not affect "Charter Members."

SYLLABUS — LESSON XII.

ELECTION OF OFFICERS.

I. NOMINATIONS.

   1. Chairman (after reading, correction, etc., of Minutes — Lesson XIV): The next business is the election of officers. Mr. A. and Miss B. will please act as Tellers. (*Tellers should promptly distribute and collect ballots.*)

   2. If there be a Nominating Committee it will now report.

   3. *Whether there be a Nominating Committee or not*—nominations from the floor are in order; (and *voting is not confined to persons nominated.*— H. M. R.)

   4. Nominations should be seconded, unless omitted by general consent.

   5. Instead of a Nominating Committee, or nominations from the floor, AN INFORMAL BALLOT (which does not elect) is the best form of nomination to avoid friction, insure free expression of the will of the Assembly, and block "close corporation" schemes.

II. ELECTIONS.

   1. Chairman (after nominations): Please prepare your ballots for President.

   2. The Tellers collect and count ballots, and hand report to Chairman.

   3. Chairman reads report, states result, and, if no election, orders another ballot.

   4. Blanks are not counted or reported.

   5. *Imperfect ballots* are counted for the person intended, in the judgment of the Tellers. *Doubtful cases* are decided by the Assembly.—CUSHING.

   6. A majority of the votes cast elects, whether the person was nominated or not, unless the Constitution, or by-laws, provides otherwise.

   7. Any eligible member may be voted for and elected on any ballot, whether receiving many or few votes, or none—on previous ballots.

   8. Officers are elected in their order, each assuming office as soon as elected, unless the Society has a rule or custom to the contrary.

   9. Secretary may be *directed to cast the vote of the Assembly* for Mr. ——, if only one is nominated. But a single objection, or one negative vote, prevents such balloting.

III. FORMS.

   1. Chairman: Nominations for President are now in order.

   2. I move we now proceed to an informal ballot for President.

   3. Chairman: Mr. B. has 7 votes; Miss C., 2; Mr. D., 8. The whole number of votes is 17; required to elect, 9. No one receiving that number, there is no election. Prepare your ballots, etc.

   4. Chairman (after reading the returns): The number of votes required to elect, 11. Mr. A. B. Jones, receiving 13 votes, is elected President. Mr. Jones will please come forward and take the Chair (except where elections occur before new term of office begins).

   5. I move the Secretary be directed to cast the vote of the Assembly for Mr. A.

   NOTE.—When elections follow Organization (Lesson XI), *only those who have complied with the conditions of membership* NOW POSSIBLE (see II, 13, on page 19) can take any part in the proceedings. If desired, the Secretary should call the roll to show who are entitled to vote.

SYLLABUS—LESSON XIII.

ORDER OF BUSINESS—SPECIAL ORDER—QUORUM.

I. ORDER OF BUSINESS, where no special order has been adopted:
   1. Calling to Order by the Chair.
   2. Reading, Correction and Approval of minutes of previous day (or meeting).
   3. Reports of Standing Committees (in their regular order).
   4. Reports of Select Committees.
   5. Unfinished Business (including all Postponed to this meeting).
   6. New Business (including business Laid on the Table at a previous meeting and now Taken from the Table — where this custom prevails).
   7. Adjourn.

II. RULES.
   1. If a Chairman rules "Adjourn" out of order till reached in the regular course, (a) Move to Adjourn; (b) If ruled out, Appeal.
   2. This secures a decision by the supreme court — the Assembly itself — and removes a source of friction. Each Assembly should settle this question for itself.
   3. If the ruling of the Chair is sustained, Adjourn can be acted on at any time, by suspending the rules — by a two-thirds vote.
   4. Business should be called for by the Chair in the regular order, but may be Laid on the Table by a majority *item by item*, but not as a whole, or as a class.
   5. *By suspension of Rules* (two-thirds vote) *any business can be taken up out of its proper order at any time*, when no other business is before the Assembly.
   6. The Secretary should furnish the Chairman with a list of committees and of all business which should come up for action at the meeting.
   7. Trustees, Boards, etc., are included in Standing Committees.
   8. Any subject made a "Special Order" for a meeting takes precedence of all other business except reading of the minutes, and can be called up at any time, even when a member has the floor.
   9. If the Chairman and Vice-Chairman are absent, the Secretary should call to order, and a Chairman *pro tem.* be at once elected.

III. FORMS.
   1. Secretary (calling to order): Will some one nominate a Chairman *pro tem.*?
   2. I move the reports of Standing Committees be Laid on the Table.
   3. The motion is out of order; only one report can be tabled in a single motion.
   4. I move to Take from the Table the resolutions on Charity Bureau work.
   5. The Chair rules that questions Taken from the Table come under New Business, and are *now* out of order.

IV. QUORUM.
   1. Unless a Quorum be present, no business is in order, except Adjourn, Recess, Fix Time, and measures the Assembly may adopt to secure a Quorum.
   2. Each Society should fix the number constituting a Quorum. In the absence of such a rule, a Quorum is a majority of the members (Committee).
   3. The presence of a Quorum, when doubted, is ascertained by calling the roll.

SYLLABUS—LESSON XIV.

MINUTES.

I. MINUTES.

1. The Chairman, at the appointed hour, should call the meeting to order and say: " The Minutes will now be read."
2. A motion to dispense with the reading of the Minutes, or any part of them (as a report, a petition), is in order.
3. Chairman: "Are there any corrections to the Minutes? (Waiting.) If not, they stand approved."
4. Corrections or amendments may be suggested by the Chairman, or any other member; and *by general consent* are made in the Minutes, by direction of the Chair.
5. If there be difference of opinion as to any proposed amendment of the Minutes, the question is put to vote—with or without a motion.
6. All corrections and amendments of Minutes are to be treated as any other Amendments—subject to debate, amendment, and other motions.
7. Any Parliamentary Question applied to an amendment does not apply to the Minutes; *e. g.* an amendment tabled does not table the Minutes.
8. There is no time limit to such amendments—*whenever an error is found* in the Minutes, *it is in order to correct it.*
9. It is not usual to formally move to approve the Minutes.
10. *Minutes should always give:*
    (*a*) Time and place of meeting;
    (*b*) Chairman and Secretary;
    (*c*) *All motions carried;* and
    (*d*) As much more as the Society wishes;
    (*e*) And be signed by the Secretary (and Chairman).
11. What more the Minutes should contain depends on the use to be made of them (published?) and the character of the Assembly. No criticism or praise should be indulged in by the Secretary.

II. FORMS.

1. Chairman: The Secretary will read the Minutes.
2. I move the reading of the Minutes be dispensed with.
3. Mr. Henry's name should be added to the Auditing Committee.
4. Chairman: The Secretary will make the change suggested.
5. Chairman: If there are no further corrections the Minutes stand approved.
6. I move all comments of the Secretary on the debates be struck out.

SYLLABUS — LESSON XV.

QUESTIONS OF PRIVILEGE — CHANGING A VOTE.

I. QUESTIONS OF PRIVILEGE :
   1. Relate to the rights and privileges of the Assembly, or of any of its members—*as members of the Assembly.*
   2. Take precedence of all questions except Fix Time, Adjourn, Recess.
   3. *If requiring immediate action :*
      (a) Take precedence of all questions.
      (b) Are in order when another has the floor.
   4. Do not require obtaining the floor, or a second.
   5. Are at once decided by the Chair.
   6. If necessary the Assembly then takes action on a motion made and seconded as usual.
   7. All subsidiary Motions apply to such a *motion on Privilege,* but do not affect the question pending when the question of Privilege was raised.
   8. All Motions and Questions of Privilege:
      (a) Can be debated.
      (b) Can be amended.
      (c) Can be reconsidered.
      (d) Need not be *finally settled,* when raised.
   9. As soon as the question of Privilege is disposed of, the question interrupted is again taken up.

II. FORMS.
   1. Mr. Chairman, I rise to a Question of Privilege.
   2. Chairman: Please state the question.
   3. The open windows admit so much noise that the speaker cannot be heard in this part of the hall.
   4. Chairman: If the Assembly wishes, the Chair will order the windows closed. (Or: The janitor will please close the windows.)
   5. I move the janitor be directed to close the windows on the south side of the hall.
   6. I move to amend the motion by inserting, after the word "close," the words "the lower half of."
   7. (*After debate, etc.*) I move the amendment be laid on the table.
   8. Chairman: It is moved and seconded to lay the amendment on the table; which would also carry the original motion to the table. Are you ready for the question?

III. CHANGING A VOTE.
   1. A member may change his vote, *before the result is fully and finally announced :* but not after such final announcement.
   2. If (a) a vote is taken by *ayes* and *noes,* (b) then a rising vote, (c) and finally the *yeas* and *nays* are ordered : a vote can be changed at any time before the result of the last vote is fully announced by the Chair.

SYLLABUS—LESSON XVI.

COMMIT AND COMMITTEES.

I. COMMITTEES.
1. Most of the effective work of Societies is done through:
   (a) *Standing Committees*, whose names, duties and powers should be fixed in the By-Laws, as well as the time and method of appointment.
   (b) *Select Committees*—appointed for special service as occasion demands.
   (c) *Committee of the Whole.*
2. Committees may be:
   (a) Nominated by a Nominating Committee.
   (b) Nominated from the floor;
   (c) Nominated by the Chair;
   (d) Appointed by the Chair.
3. Committees are elected by ayes and noes unless otherwise ordered.
4. The Chair "appoints" a Committee by simply naming its members, but "nominates" by naming and *taking a vote*.
5. It is usually best to have the Chair appoint Committees.

II. TO COMMIT. RULES.
1. "Commit" is debatable and opens the main question to debate.
2. Can be amended by
   (a) Altering }
   (b) Instructing } the Committee.
3. "Commit" may be moved alone, leaving the kind of Committee to be settled afterwards.
4. One motion may include all these points; *e. g.* "I move the petition be referred to the Library Committee, with instructions, etc."
5. If different Committees are suggested, votes should be taken on:
   (a) Committee of the Whole;
   (b) Standing Committee;
   (c) Select Committee.
6. The Secretary should notify each member of the Committee, and give Chairman of Committee all papers and instructions, and, if a Special Committee, a list of its members.
7. The first person named is Chairman until the Committee meets; and permanently, unless at its first meeting the Committee elects another Chairman.
8. Each Committee can appoint Sub-committees, which report only to the appointing Committee.

III. FORMS.
1. I move the proposal be referred to the Trustees.
2. I move the Club resolve itself into a Committee of the Whole on renting a hall.
3. I move to amend (the motion to commit) by instructing the Committee, etc.
4. I move to amend the instructions by inserting after——the words ——.
5. Chairman: Of how many shall the Committee consist?

etc.

et cetera

SYLLABUS — LESSON XVII.

ADJOURN, UNQUALIFIED — ADJOURN, QUALIFIED.

I. ADJOURN (UNQUALIFIED):
1. Precedes all questions except Fix Time to which to Adjourn (Privileged).
2. While Adjourn is pending the following questions are in order:
   (a) Withdrawal of Motion to Adjourn.
   (b) Enter " Reconsider " on Minutes.
   (c) To Fix Time (Privileged).
   (d) Motion as to how vote shall be taken.
   (Also, *if requiring immediate action :*)
   (e) Appeals.
   (f) Parliamentary Inquiries.
   (g) Questions of Order.
   (h) Questions of Privilege.
3. Cannot be Amended, Debated or Reconsidered.
4. Can be renewed after other business, or progress in debate.
   Forms. I move to adjourn. The ayes have it, and we stand adjourned (to 8 P. M.).

II. ADJOURN (QUALIFIED) — FIVE FORMS.
1. To Adjourn *sine die.* When Adjourn, *whatever form the motion may have,* has the effect of dissolving the Assembly, it *loses all privilege : can be debated, amended, tabled,* etc.—H. M. R. AND REED.
2. To Adjourn *at* a time.
3. To Adjourn *to* a time.
4. To Adjourn *to* a place.
5. Any desired combination of 1, 2, 3, 4.
6. Adjourn (qualified) has no privilege and precedes nothing.
7. Can be debated and amended.
8. Yields to all Privileged, Incidental and Subsidiary Questions, except Postpone Indefinitely, and Object to Consideration.
9. Can be Reconsidered, except affirmative vote on 1, 3, 4.

III. FORMS.
1. I move that we Adjourn *sine die* (or, *without day*) at 5 P. M.
2. I move we Adjourn to meet at 10 A. M., July 6th.
3. I move we adjourn at 9 P. M., to meet at the Elgin Opera House, at 7 P. M., September 23d.
4. The ayes have it, and the Club will adjourn at 9 P. M., etc.
5. (*At the time fixed.*) The time for adjournment has come, and the Club stands adjourned to 7 P. M., September 23d, at the Elgin, etc.

SYLLABUS — LESSON XVIII.

RECONSIDER — (More Fully Treated).

I. Reconsider.

1. If any Assembly wishes to modify or annul any action already taken, the usual course is to Reconsider.

2. "Reconsider" must be moved (except where vote was by ballot) by one who voted on the prevailing side, whether majority or minority; *e. g.* If 18 vote for and 12 against Previous Question (requiring two-thirds vote) one of the 12 must move to Reconsider.

3. Where the vote was by ballot, any member may move to Reconsider.

4. Any member can second Reconsider.

5. Must be moved on the day on which the vote to be Reconsidered was taken, or on the next day; legal holidays not counting.

6. To Reconsider a debatable question is debatable, and opens the main question to debate.

7. "Reconsider" needs only a majority of the votes cast, even when the question reconsidered requires two-thirds, or a still larger vote.

II. Effect and Order of Reconsideration.

1. An Amendment, if voted on, must be reconsidered before an amendment to this amendment can be Reconsidered.

2. The main question, if voted on, must be Reconsidered before an amendment can be Reconsidered.

3. *General Rule.* No vote can be Reconsidered, *without first Reconsidering— in inverse order* — all subsequent votes which affect the question to be Reconsidered. Example: (If amendments and resolution have been voted on:) *Before an amendment to an amendment can be Reconsidered, Reconsider must be carried* (1) on the resolution; (2) on the amendment— *then* (3) the amendment to the amendment can be Reconsidered.

4. *Reconsider, lost,* leaves the main question as it was before Reconsider was moved.

5. *Reconsider, carried,* places the question reconsidered again before the Assembly, just as it stood before it was voted on.

6. The effect of *moving to Reconsider* is to suspend all action required by the original motion, till Reconsider is acted on, or lapses by passing the time limit.

7. Reconsider may be "moved and entered on the minutes" for future action, whatever question is pending, *even while another has the floor.*

III. Forms.

1. I move to Reconsider the (vote on the) amendment (to the amendment).

2. The *ayes* have it and the amendment is again before the Assembly.

3. I move to Reconsider the vote on the Prohibition Platform, and wish the motion entered on the Minutes.

Note.—For list of questions which can not be Reconsidered, see page 7.

·

SYLLABUS — LESSON XIX.

FIX TIME (AND PLACE) TO WHICH TO ADJOURN.

I. To FIX TIME is:
  1. Privileged—if made when another question is pending.
  2. Unprivileged—if made when no other question is pending.

II. FIX TIME, PRIVILEGED—(*i. e. made when another question is pending*):
  1. Precedes all other questions: is in order while Adjourn is pending, and *even after it is voted to adjourn*, before the result is fully stated.
  2. Can not be debated.
  3. Can be amended, but no other Subsidiary motion applies to it.
  4. Can be Reconsidered.
  5. Can not be made while another has the floor.
  6. While Fix Time is pending, to enter Reconsider on the minutes, is in order: also the following questions, *if requiring immediate action:*
      (*a*) Appeals.
      (*b*) Motions as to Mode of Voting.
      (*c*) Parliamentary Inquiries.
      (*d*) Points of Order.
      (*e*) Questions of Privilege.
      (*f*) Withdrawal of Motion to Fix Time.

III. FORMS.
  1. I move that when we adjourn we adjourn to (meet at) 9 A. M., August 4th.
  2. *Entry in Minutes.* "On motion of Mr. A., the Club fixed the time to which to adjourn at 9 A. M., August 4th."

IV. FIX TIME, UNPRIVILEGED—(*i. e. made when no other question is pending*):
  1. Is a Principal Motion, and yields to the usual Parliamentary questions.
  2. Precedes nothing.
  3. Can be Debated, Amended and Reconsidered.
  4. The Forms are the same as in Fix Time Privileged.

  NOTE A.—Avoid if possible combining "Fix Time" with "Adjourn"; *e. g.* "I move to adjourn to 7 P. M." The best plan is first to Fix the Time, and then "Adjourn" will find the Assembly prepared.

  NOTE B.—*Fix the Place to which to Adjourn* is Privileged or Unprivileged, just as Fix Time is: and all the above rules apply equally to this motion. —H. M. R. Or *Time and Place* can both be fixed in one motion; *e. g.* "I move that when we adjourn we adjourn to meet at the Temple, on November 10th, at 8 P. M."

SYLLABUS — LESSON XX.

EXTEND, LIMIT, AND CLOSE DEBATE.

I. EXTEND, LIMIT AND CLOSE DEBATE :
  1. Apply to all debatable questions.
  2. Rank next below the Previous Question.—II. M. R.
  3. Require a two-thirds vote.
  4. Can be Amended and Reconsidered, by a majority vote.
  5. Can not be debated.
  6. Unless limited by the mover, Apply to a motion and its amendments.

II. LIMIT DEBATE—May Limit:
  1. The length of each speech (to five minutes).
  2. The number of speeches (to two on each side).
  3. The whole debate (to 30 minutes—*which is really "closing debate"* in 30 minutes).
  4. FORM. I move debate be limited to one-minute speeches.

III. CLOSE DEBATE :
  1. Closes Debate *at* a time, or *in* a certain time.
  2. When the time fixed for closing debate comes, this motion has the same effect as the Previous Question, *i. e.* cuts off debate and amendments, and brings the pending question or questions to vote.

IV. FORMS.
  1. I move that debate be now closed.
  2. I move to amend by striking out the words "now closed" and inserting the words "closed in ten minutes" (or "closed at 2 P. M.").
  3. (*At the time fixed*) Chairman: The time for closing debate has come, and the question before us is on the adoption of the resolutions on Temperance. Are you ready for the question?

V. EXTEND DEBATE—May Apply to:
  1. The length of a single speech, or of all speeches.
  2. The times a member or members may speak.
  3. The whole time fixed for debate—on the program, or by vote.

VI. FORMS.
  1. I move the member be allowed five minutes to finish his speech
  2. I move the time for consideration of this report be extended to 11:30.

SYLLABUS — LESSON XXI.

THE PREVIOUS QUESTION (More Fully Stated) — PREVIOUS QUESTION AND RECONSIDER.

I. The Previous Question:
  1. Means: *Stop debating, stop amending, and vote.*
  2. Applies to all debatable questions, and no others.
  3. If Laid on the Table, carries the main question with it.
  4. Its effect is to bring the pending question or questions to an immediate vote.
  5. It can not be debated, or amended, postponed or committed.
  6. Previous Question, ordered on Commit or Amend, applies to the main question also, *unless limited by the mover of the Previous Question.*
  7. Previous Question, ordered on the following questions, does not affect the main question:
    (*a*) Appeals.
    (*b*) Postpone Definitely.
    (*c*) Postpone Indefinitely.
    (*d*) Questions of Privilege.
    (*e*) Reconsider.

II. Previous Question and Reconsider.
  1. *Previous Question, lost,* can be Reconsidered.
  2. *Previous Question, carried,* can be Reconsidered before voting under it begins.
  3. While Previous Question is in force, any vote taken under it can be Reconsidered, subject to the Previous Question; *i. e.* without debate or amendment.
  4. When votes have been taken on all questions to which it applies, the Previous Question is exhausted, and has no further effect on any question.
  5. After Previous Question is exhausted, votes previously taken under it, if Reconsider is moved on them, are treated as if Previous Question had never been ordered.

III. Forms.
  1. I move the Previous Question (on the amendment).
  2. The question before the Assembly is, Shall the main question be now put? All in favor, etc.
  3. Shall the question be now put on the amendment?
  4. The ayes have it and the Previous Question is ordered (on the amendment).

SYLLABUS—LESSON XXII.

SUSPEND RULES, BY-LAWS, CONSTITUTION, ETC.

I. To Suspend Constitution and By-Laws.

   1. No Assembly has the power to suspend the Constitution, or any part of it— even by a unanimous vote.

   2. The By-Laws can not be suspended, except where they provide by a special rule for the suspension of one or more specified By-Laws.

   3. Care should be taken to include in the Constitution and By-Laws only such Rules as an Assembly will never need to suspend.

   4. If Constitution or By-Laws contain orders *in the nature of Rules, it should be allowed* to suspend them; *e. g.* the Time of Meeting, Order of Business, etc.

II. To Suspend Rules of Order.

   1. Certain Rules of Order can be suspended by a two-thirds vote, for a definite object, stated in the motion to Suspend.

   2. No Rules involving Parliamentary Law or Principles can be suspended.— H. M. R.

     (*a*) An undebatable question can not be made debatable, by suspension of Rules.

     (*b*) An unamendable question can not be made amendable, by suspending the Rules.

     (*c*) The Order of Precedence of Motions can not be changed by suspension.

     (*d*) Rules as to the Rights of Chairman, Secretary or members, can not be suspended.

   3. It is in order, by a two-thirds vote, to Suspend Rules and —

     (*a*) Allow visitors the right to debate, *but not to vote.*

     (*b*) *Change the hour* for Closing Debate on a subject, or for Recess, etc.

     (*c*) Take up any particular business out of its proper order.

   4. " Suspend Rules " can not be Reconsidered, Amended or Debated.

   5. Can not be renewed for the same purpose at the *same meeting.*

   6. Can be Laid on the Table.

   7. Rules passed by a superior, cannot be suspended by a subordinate, body.

   8. No rule conferring rights on one-third or less of the members, can be suspended, except by *unanimous vote*, or general consent.

III. Forms.

   1. I move to Suspend the Rules and take up the resolutions on Municipal Reform.

   2. I move to Suspend the Rules and allow the delegation from the Bureau of Charities to take part in the debate.

   3. The *ayes* have it, the rules are suspended, and the question before us is on the adoption of the resolutions, etc. Are you ready, etc.?

IV. Standing Rules:

   1. May be suspended at any time by a majority vote.

SYLLABUS — LESSON XXIII.

TO AMEND CONSTITUTION, BY-LAWS, RULES OF ORDER, AND STANDING RULES.

I. CONSTITUTION, BY-LAWS AND RULES OF ORDER:
  1. Can be amended only at a regular (stated) business meeting.
  2. Written notice of the proposed amendment must be given at a previous regular (stated) business meeting.
  3. An amendment to Rules of Order, Constitution, By-Laws (adopted and in force) is really a Principal Motion, subject to an amendment and an amendment to the amendment.—H. M. R.
  4. Such amendments to the proposed amendment to Rules of Order, etc., *must be strictly* GERMANE.
  5. To amend Rules of Order, etc., requires two-thirds of those *present and voting.*
  6. But this amendment, *before adoption as a part of the Rules, etc.,* can be amended by a majority.

II. STANDING RULES include orders the society can adopt, amend, rescind or suspend—by a mere majority, at any meeting, without previous notice.

III. HIGHER LAWS.
  1. Constitution, By-Laws and Rules must conform to U. S. and State Laws, and to the Rules and Orders of Superior Bodies (Ecclesiastical, Fraternal, etc.).
  2. No Subordinate Society can amend laws enacted by its Superior.
  3. Where the Society is to own property, it should be Incorporated, and a member of Committee on Constitution should consult a lawyer, so that the *Constitution and By-Laws shall conform to State Laws: including laws as to* AMENDMENT OF CONSTITUTION AND BY-LAWS, which *must be observed.*

IV. FORMS.
  1. The usual forms of amend apply.
  2. Written notice should give the present rule, proposed change and rule as amended.

    NOTE.—Societies usually prescribe methods for amending their Constitution, By-Laws, Rules of Order and Standing Rules. Where not so provided for, the common Parliamentary Law, as here given, regulates such action.

SYLLABUS — LESSON XXIV.

HOW TO REVERSE ACTION ON AMENDMENTS.

I. *If a motion to* INSERT *certain words is* LOST — *The Assembly:*
  1. Can not insert the same words, or part of them.
  2. Can insert (part of) the same words and strike out other words.
  3. Can insert the same words (or part of them) with added words.

II. *If a motion to* INSERT *certain words is* CARRIED — *The Assembly:*
  1. Can not strike out the inserted words, or part of them.
  2. Can not strike out (part of) the inserted words, and insert other words.
  3. Can strike out the inserted words (or part of them) *with other words.*
  4. Can strike out (part of) the inserted words, with added words, and insert other words.

III. *If a motion to* STRIKE OUT *certain words is* LOST — *The Assembly:*
  1. Can not strike out the same words, or part of them.
  2. Can strike out the same words (or part of them) with added words.
  3. Can strike out the same words (or part of them) and insert other words.
  4. Can strike out (part of) the same words, with added words, and insert others.

IV. *If a motion to* STRIKE OUT *certain words is* CARRIED — *The Assembly:*
  1. Can not insert the same words, or part of them.
  2. Can not strike out other words, and insert (part of) the same words.
  3. Can insert the same words (or part of them) with added words.
  4. Can S. O. other words and insert (part of) the same words with added words.

V. *If a motion to* STRIKE OUT *certain words* AND INSERT *other words is* LOST — IT can be RENEWED *if* EITHER SET *of words* (*i. e.* if either the words to be struck out, or the words to be inserted) *is* CHANGED:
  1. To (part of) the same words, with added words.   3. To other words.
  2. To part of the same words.   4. To nothing.
  EXAMPLES: S. O. *ab* and insert *cd* (lost). (1) Can S. O. *abx* and insert *cd*; (2) Can S. O. *a* and insert *cd*; (3) Can S. O. *ab* and insert *xy*; (4) Can S. O. *ab*.

VI. *If a motion to* STRIKE OUT *certain words* AND INSERT *others is* CARRIED — IT can be REVERSED *only when* EACH SET *of words is* CHANGED:
  1. To same words (*or part of them*) with added words.
  2. To other words.
  3. To different words, or nothing (*i. e.* when one set of words is *changed,* as in 1 or 2; and the other set is omitted).
  EXAMPLES: S. O. *ab* and insert *cd* (carried). (1) Can S. O. (*a*)*bx* and insert (*c*)*dy*; (2) Can S. O. *x* and insert (*c*)*dy*; (3) Can S. O. *abx* or *bx* (but not *a* or *ab*), and insert nothing: OR, Can insert *cy* or *cdy* (but not *c* or *cd*), and S. O. nothing.

VII. GENERAL LAWS ON REVERSING ACTION. (R. R., REED AND CUSHING.)
  1. Things done must stay done—unless Reconsidered.
  2. A motion (or amendment), *to be in order, must be* SUBSTANTIALLY DIFFERENT from any motion (or amendment) already acted on by the Assembly, during the Session.
  3. "SUBSTANTIAL DIFFERENCE" means *more than a mere change of* WORDS.

NOTE A.—"The same words" means *words inserted* (or struck out) *in one motion.*
NOTE B.—"Added words" may be added or inserted by another motion *for the sole purpose* of making reversal possible.

INDEX.

	PAGE
Abbreviations	11
Adjourn	44
" at a certain time . .	44
" fix place to which to .	48
" " time " " " (priv'd)	48
" " " " " (unpriv'd)	48
" order of business and .	36
" qualified . . .	44
" unqualified . . .	44
" sine die . . .	44
" to a certain place . .	44
" " " time . .	44
Amend, 14, 16, 22, 28, 30, 38, 46, 56, 58	
" by adding . . . 14, 58	
" amendments . . .	16
" " to amendments	16
" by-laws, constitution, etc.	56
" by consent of second .	26
" " general consent . .	26
" " division . . .	28
" forms of . . 14, 28, 30	
" germane . . 14, 30, 56	
" hostile	14
" by inserting . . . 14, 58	
" minutes	38
" motions not amendable .	16
" reconsidering . . . 22, 46	
" reversing action on . .	58
" rules of order . .	56
" " of a superior body .	56
" separate amendments .	16
" standing rules . . .	56
" by striking out . 14, 30, 58	
" " " " and inserting 14, 30, 58	
" substitute . . . 14, 30	
" tabling	20
" trivial	14
" voting on, order of . .	16

	PAGE
Appeal	24
" chairman voting on .	24
" tie-vote on . . .	24
Ayes and noes, voting by . .	12
Ballot 22, 34	
" informal . . .	34
Business, order of . . .	36
By-laws, amend . . .	56
" suspend . . .	54
Calling meeting to order . . 12, 36	
Chairman, absence of . .	36
" how address . .	12
" when can he vote .	24
Changing a vote . . .	40
Close debate 18, 50	
Commit	42
Committee of the whole . .	42
Committees, standing, select .	42
" sub- . . .	42
Consideration, objection to .	18
Constitution, adopt, etc. . .	32
" amend . . . 32, 56	
" and "charter members"	32
" suspend . .	54
Corporations	56
Debate, close 18, 50	
" extend and limit . .	50
Division, amend by . . . 14, 28	
" call for . . .	16
" questions not subject to	28
Doubting a vote . . .	16
Election of officers . . . 12, 34	
" " committees . .	42
Extend debate	50
Fix time (and place) to which to adjourn	48
Forms of motions, etc., see various lessons.	
Germane, amendments must be 14, 56	

	PAGE
Higher laws	54, 56
Hostile, amendments may be .	14
Incidental questions . . .	11
Informal ballot . . .	34
Lay on the table . . .	20
Limit debate	50
Minutes, amend, correct, approve	38
" should contain . .	38, 48
Motions, making and seconding .	12
" lists of . . .	9, 11
" (see questions)	
Nominations . . .	12, 34, 42
" by informal ballot .	34
Objection to consideration . .	18
Obtaining the floor . . .	12
Officers, election of . . .	12, 34
Order of business . . .	36
" point of	12
Organization, permanent . .	32
" temporary .	12, 32
Parliamentary inquiry . .	16
Point of order	12
Postpone, indefinitely . .	22
" to a certain time. .	22
Previous question . .	14, 52
" " and reconsider.	52
Principal motions . . .	18
Privilege, questions of . .	40
Privileged questions . . .	11
Questions of privilege . .	40
" incidental . . .	11
" privileged . . .	11
" subsidiary . . .	11
" undebatable . .	9
" can not be amended .	16
" " " laid on table	20
" " " reconsidered	9
Quorum	36
Recess	20
Recognition by the chair . .	12
Reconsider . . .	22, 46
" and previous question	52
" questions which can not be reconsidered .	9

	PAGE
Resolutions, how to offer . .	12
" write, read, hand to chair, etc. . .	12
Reverse action on amendments .	58
Rules of order, to amend . .	56
" " " to suspend . .	54
" " a superior body .	36, 54, 56
Second, consent of, to amendment	26
" " " " withdrawal	26
Seconding motions . . .	12
Secretary calls meeting to order	36
" counts votes . .	16
Special order	36
Standing rules, to amend, etc. .	56
" " to suspend. .	54
Subsidiary questions . . .	11
Substitute	14, 30
" must be germane (note)	30
" when not in order .	30
Suspend by-laws and constitution	54
" rules of order and standing rules . . .	36, 54
" rules of a superior body	36, 54
Take from the table . . .	20
Take up business out of proper order	36
Tellers	16, 34
Trivial amendments, rule out .	14
Trustees	36
Undebatable questions. See TABLES.	9
Unfinished business . . .	22, 36
Vote, changing a . . .	40
" doubting a . . .	16
" when can chair (note) .	24
" who can	34, 40
Voting . . .	12, 16, 34, 42
" order of, on amendments	16
" by ayes and noes . .	12
" by ballot . . .	34
" by division . . .	16
" by yeas and nays (note) .	24
Withdrawal of motions . .	26
Yeas and nays (note) . . .	24

LITERARY STUDIES.

THIS SERIES OF LITERARY STUDIES COM-
PRISES THREE OF DR. MATHEWS' MOST
POPULAR BOOKS. THEY DEAL WITH
THEMES WHICH WILL INTEREST AND
THEY FURNISH HELPFUL SUGGESTIONS
AS WELL AS VALUABLE LITERARY AND
HISTORICAL INFORMATION.

Oratory and Orators.

*The Beginnings of Oratory, The Qualifi-
cations of the Orator, The Political and
Pulpit Orators of Various Countries —
these and kindred topics are ably presented.*

"It is a volume that no student can
read without benefiting from it."— *Boston
Transcript.*

"It will attract the closest attention
from all thoughtful politicians, states-
men, and clergymen. Besides the value
of the directions to the public speaker,
the book abounds with sparkling anec-
dotes, and gems of thought from cele-
brated orators."—*Philadelphia Record.*

"The author treats in a suggestive and
fascinating strain all the great English,
Irish and American authors, analyzing
their respective styles with a subtlety
which shows profound research and well
balanced judgment."—*Boston Traveler.*

"No better idea of the great orators,
whose names are in all men's mouths can
be found than from Dr. Mathews' glow-
ing pages."—*Philadelphia Inquirer.*

Words: Their Use and Abuse.

*A study of the significance of words,
classification of words, common impro-
prieties of speech, etc.*

"A book that will lead to the reforma-
tion of thousands of careless talkers."—
Christian Union.

"No one can turn to a single page of
the book without finding something worth
remembering. It is a book both for
libraries and general reading. Scholars
will not disdain its many valuable illus-
trations, while the rising writer will find
in it a perfect wealth of rules and suggestions to help him form a good style of
expression."—*The Publishers' Weekly.*

"It gives the condensed wisdom of
every man who ever handled the subject."—*Catholic Mirror.*

Hours with Men and Books.

*A series of talks about men of letters,
books, and subjects of literary interest.*

"A store-house of valuable information."—*London Morning Post, Eng.*

"A book that encourages the love of
letters is so rare that it is impossible not
to be grateful to Dr. Mathews for one that
is so kindly and attractive."— *Atlantic
Monthly.*

"Any one desirous of cultivating an
acquaintance with the leading thinkers
and actors of all ages and to have in a
compendious form, intelligent opinions
on their lives and works, will find herein
the result of deep research and sound
reflection."—*Sheffield Post, Eng.*

"Calculated to impart knowledge in
concrete form which hours of study
would not give."— *Banker and Trades-
man, Boston.*

---

*3 Vols. in a box, handsomely bound in cloth
and illustrated. Price, $5.00.*

SCOTT, FORESMAN & CO.,

PUBLISHERS,

378-388 Wabash Avenue,   Chicago.